Immigration and Family Law

An Attorney's Toolbox of Best Practices

By Connie Kaplan, Esq.

Additional copies are available at special quantity discounts for bulk purchases for sales promotions, premiums, fundraising, and educational use.

For more information, please contact:

The Law Office of Connie Kaplan, P.A. **954-357-0957**

Contact the author directly at ck@conniekaplanlawyer.com

Thank you for your interest in learning more about how to help your clients.

We are available to help advise you and your clients on more complicated immigration matters.

Call today to learn more

Case Evaluation

954-357-0957

Table of Contents

Immigration and Family Law

An Attorney's Toolbox of Best Practices

From the Desk of Connie Kaplan, Immigration Attorney

Family Law & Immigration Partners

Our country is the entry point of many, many ethnicities comprising of a patchwork of interesting cultures and lifestyles. As attorneys, we do all we can to serve our clients' needs within our lawful niches, but the truth is that few situations are tidy and neat, free of any additional complicating factors. By its very nature, the marriage between family law and immigration law raises many questions that require answers, but that also offers opportunities for all of us to offer our clients superior and more holistic lawful services.

Most Americans have little to no idea what it feels like to be in a new unfamiliar country. And they know even less about the winding maze and complications involved in gaining lawful residency in the United States.

As an immigrant, I do know.

For 16 years, I sought a way to permanent residency and experienced heart-wrenching rejection for my asylum and other immigration requests. I even endured deportation or, as it known in the immigration community, removal proceedings. Like those who visit my office, I agonized through trying to understand everything. And despite my attempts to take the right steps at the right times, I made all the mistakes that my clients make today before they ever walk into my office.

Like my clients, I KNOW what is like to worry about safety, and to chase after security, especially when most of the options or choices are not within their control.

In these pages I aim to take what I have learned both as an immigrant myself and as a family immigration attorney and share with you nuances that I hope will provide a toolbox that will undoubtedly serve you and your clients in a more specialized way. By adding a few simple questions to your client intake process and by understanding a few concepts and details of the law, you will become an even more powerful champion for your family law clients who also share immigration challenges. Imagine being able to help a family learn that they have options they have not even dreamed of or to help solve a problem in a way that may have never occurred to you before.

This book illuminates the differences between family law matters when the family law attorney does not dig any deeper than the surface in representing his or her clients, and when the family law attorney is better informed.

What I hear over and over from family law attorneys is that they "do not really have clients from the immigrant population". In most cases, I hear back from them a few months after we talk or after my presentation on this topic, only to have them reveal that they service more clients with immigration questions than they previously thought, and that before they were simply not asking the right questions assuming it was not an issue. This is very common. I am hoping to change it.

Difficult, if not impossible, to overcome consequences may result when attorneys represent persons who are living in the US and are unaware of the immigration consequences of family law lawful advice. This is the result when they do not even think to ask the question: "Is either of you not a US citizen?"

On the other hand, when the family law attorney establishes questions about immigration status and adds them to their client intake, the attorney can spot issues and change the conversation with clients.

Each chapter discusses a different scenario where family law and immigration law intersect. Practice tips for the family law practitioner are also included.

Keep in mind that this book references Florida's Family law and immigration law as of February 2019. The latter is constantly changing. Moreover, the practice of immigration law is also heavily affected by executive orders, regulations, and the enforcement priorities of the current administration.

One

Understanding US Immigration

There is not one specific agency for immigration, in fact, there are many agencies and departments that foreign nationals may have to interact with throughout their process. Knowing where to turn depends on the person's situation and its complexity.

The first step for a foreign-born national may be to secure a visa to initially enter the United States. The Department of State (DOS) issues the visas through our embassies and consulates. There are many kinds of visas and each has a specific purpose. Visas are limited in duration. For example, the usual duration of stay on a (B1/B2) visitor visa is six months.

Sometimes foreign visitors decide they want to remain in the US permanently. Often, US companies seek foreign nationals to fill positions with specific skills. They may sponsor a foreign national through a multi-step process. Generally, but not always, the process towards lawful permanent residency based on employment begins with the Department of Labor (DOL). If the labor certification is approved, the employer will need to file a petition with US Citizenship and Immigration Services (CIS), which is an agency within the department of Homeland Security (DHS). When approved, the employee may need to apply for a visa at the consulate, so then again DOS is involved. When the USCIS petition is denied, the employer may appeal.

The US Department of Homeland Security oversees Immigration Service Centers that are set up around the country to address specific types of immigration cases. Local field offices are where foreign nationals have their fingerprints taken or where they attend the interview as part of their application process.

Many of the immigrants living in the US unlawfully or without documents arrived here lawfully and never left. After their approved stay ended, they simply remained. Those undocumented people may be in "removal proceedings" or what is commonly referred to as deportation. They must argue in front of an immigration judge as to why they should be permitted to stay in the US despite having broken the law with the unauthorized presence. The immigration courts are not independent; rather, the US Department of Justice through its Executive Office of Immigration Review (EOIR) oversees the immigration courts.

Talking the Immigration Talk

Learning the Terms

In this section you will find terms commonly used to discuss various immigration issues. The more you understand, the more the concepts will become familiar to you so that you feel more confident about tackling your clients' immigration matter. Family matters, including marriages, siblings, children and custody, and relationships — all present unique and complex situations when considering divorce for or adoption of foreign nationals.

As you read, you will begin to have even more questions. Keep paper and pen next to you so that you can write down any questions about what you are reading, or you can write the questions right in the margin to remember what sparked it. You will be prepared and ready to learn how you can help your client move forward.

Follow along as I help you get up to speed on the vocabulary used by these agencies in documents, in communications, and in the courts.

Affidavit of Support

When a US citizen or a Lawful Permanent Resident (LPR) sponsors a foreign national family member — such as a spouse, parent, or child — the sponsor must guarantee support for that prospective immigrant should he or she become unable to pay for their own care. This contract is with the federal government and is called an Affidavit of Support (Form I-864). Even if the couple divorces, the US citizen or LPR spouse is still liable.

An Affidavit of Support is dissolved only when:

- **The foreign national can prove 40 quarters or 10 years of work;**
- **The foreign national or his or her sponsor dies; or**
- **The foreigner becomes a US citizen.**

Becoming a sponsor for a foreign national family member is a significant commitment. These contracts are taken seriously by Immigration and are enforced.

USCIS

In our context, United States Citizenship and Immigration Services is the federal agency responsible for determining familial relationship and the good faith of a marriage when that forms the basis for a petition for an immigration benefit. USCIS reviews applications and determines if the couple's actions demonstrate they entered their marriage in good faith, in other words, did the couple intend to truly build a life together?

What Will USCIS Look For?

USCIS will investigate and review the actions the couple took before they ever got married and naturally, after the marriage too.

- **Did the couple join all their financial responsibilities?**
- **Did they open bank accounts together? Mortgages?**

- **Were both individuals on joint plans for health insurance? Life insurance?**
- **Did they share cell phone plans, tenancies?**
- **Do they have children together?**

Combined with traceable proofs, the answers to these questions are compelling stories indicating the couple truly intended to secure a happy life and future together.

Authorized Stay

Foreign nationals who have lawfully applied for some consideration such as an extension or change of immigration status or deferred action, are given permission to be in the US for a specific timeframe, called Period of Authorized Stay by the Attorney General. During this time, the foreign national does not accrue any unlawful presence.

Unlawful presence is any period in the US without admission, parole, or authorized stay. With some limited exceptions, a period that is not authorized and leading to unlawful presence would create specific bars to inadmissibility (not permitted to reenter the US) for.

These inadmissibility bars are:

- **3 years, if departing the US after having accrued more than 180 days but less than 1 year of unlawful presence during a single stay and before the commencement of removal proceedings;**

- 10 years, if departing the US after having accrued one year or more of unlawful presence during a single stay, regardless of whether the foreign national left before, during, or after removal proceedings; or

- Permanently, if reentering or try to reenter the US without being admitted or paroled after having accrued more than one year of unlawful presence in the aggregate during one or more stays in the United States.

Board of Immigration Appeals

This administrative appellate body is a part of the United States Department of Justice. The BIA role is to weigh appeals and decisions relative to immigration applications. Decisions rendered from the BIA are often cited when deciding asylum applications.

Certified Translation

Foreign nationals who apply for any immigration benefit must submit documents showing eligibility (such as relationship, education, persecution, etc.). Since these documents are in a language other than English, they must include a certified translation.

A Certified Translation is an accompanying document revealing the translation and the translator's credentials, and it must be notarized.

In most cases, if the translation is done abroad, a Hague apostille is also needed.

Derived Citizenship

Children may derive citizenship through a parent, both parents, and sometimes grandparents, often without the child's knowledge. There are several ways for minors to derive citizenship, one of which being the Child Citizenship Act of 2000.

The Child Citizenship Act allows foreign-born children to acquire US citizenship automatically when:

- **At least one of the parents is a US citizen by birth or naturalization;**
- **The child is under age 18; and**
- **The child is or has resided in the United States in both legal *and* physical custody of the US citizen parent.**

Immediate Relative

In understanding family immigration in the US, there are two categories of foreign family members, each carrying its own specific criteria that determines what the foreign family members can expect when applying for a visa. These categories are: Immediate Relative and Family Preference.

To qualify as an *immediate relative*, the foreign national must be:

- **The spouse of a US citizen;**
- **A person who is under 21 years of age who is the child of a US citizen;**
- **A person who is an orphan who has been adopted abroad by a US citizen;**
- **An orphan who WILL BE adopted in the US by a US citizen; or**
- **The parent of a US citizen who is at least 21 years old.**

As an "immediate relative" the foreign national will not need to wait in line for a visa to become available to be able to immigrate or to change status from within the US, because there are an unlimited number of visas available to those who belong in this category.

For example, if a US citizen married a foreign national while visiting or living abroad, and he or she is now anticipating returning to the US and wants the spouse to join him or her, the spouse would be considered an immediate relative.

Family Preference

Unlike the "Immediate Relative" category, those qualifying only under Family Preference must wait in line for a visa to become available because the visas for Family Preference are NOT unlimited in number.

Three things need to happen before the family under preference categories may come to the US: 1. an initial petition must be filed; 2. that petition needs to be approved, and 3. a visa must then become available. Only at that time, these family applicants may complete the process of applying for permanent residency in the US.

The following categories are considered Family Preference:

- **Sons and daughters of US citizens and their spouses and minor children;**
- **Brothers and sisters of US citizens, and their spouses and minor children, provided the US citizen sponsor is at least 21 years of age; and**
- **Spouses, minor children, and unmarried sons and daughters (age 21 and over) of LPRs.**

Individuals fall under the "children" category if they are under 21 years of age, and under "sons and daughters" if over 21.

Priority Date

When foreign nationals file a petition, the date the petition is received is known as the priority date. Each month, a visa bulletin is released by the DOS reflecting which priority date is current for that month. A foreign national's priority date *must* be current before the foreigner files the application for residency.

Permanent Residency

When US citizens and their foreign spouses have been married *longer than two years* at the time of approval, the foreign national will receive ***Lawful Permanent Residence*** (and is therefore an ***LPR, a lawful*** *permanent resident).*   This is evidenced by a permanent green card. We will use "green card" and "permanent residency" interchangeably.

However, the US Government tests the good faith of marriages between US citizens and their foreign spouses with conditional status. When they have been married for *less than two years* at the time of approval, the foreign national becomes only a **Conditional Permanent Resident** (or a **CPR**). This is evidenced by a conditional green card.

Before the end of those two years arrives, the couple must again prove that the marriage is in good faith, so that the conditions on the green cards may be removed.

If the couple splits for any reason and the marriage is not working out, the timing is important.

Some pertinent questions are:

- **Are they legally separated? (not all states have this as an option)**
- **Is the couple no longer living together?**
- **Are they on a trial separation while seeking counseling to salvage the marriage?**
- **Has a divorce been filed or is the divorce already final?**

How your client answers these questions affects the foreign spouse's status in the US. This is especially critical before advising the client to start the divorce proceeding.

The world has grown smaller. More US citizens travel today, and more people are marrying outside their faith, ethnicity, and country. With immigration occupying so much of the sentiments and news today, tougher scrutiny has become part of the process in our country. According to immigration law, married couples must show that at the time they got married the marriage was in good faith and both individuals intended to build a life together.

Removal of Conditions

When a foreign spouse who is married to a US citizen receives residency prior to reaching the two-year anniversary, he or she must apply for removal of conditions within the 90-day period prior to the expiration of the green card.

Naturalization

Naturalization is the process by which foreign nationals may become US citizens.

Visa

There are 185 different types of US Visas, each falling into one of two categories: immigrant visas and nonimmigrant visas.

When people who reside in foreign countries want to come to the United States, they must generally obtain a US visa, a travel document placed in the traveler's passport by the US Department of States through its embassies and consulates. Each visa carries a specific purpose and a limited timeline.

The visa allows a foreign national to travel to a US port of entry and ask for admission into the country; it is not a guarantee of admission and it does not bind the US government.

Two

Divorce and Immigration

When a family law attorney prepares a client for divorce and does not discuss either of the spouses' immigration status, advising the client of the best course of action is limited to the facts known. This lack of information could lead the attorney to cause financial harm for the client by advising a separation or divorce.

For example, there are situations where if the couple agrees to continue to live together, the US citizen who is married to a foreign-born spouse could benefit financially by limiting his or her liability. Likewise, if they divorce right away, the foreign national spouse may either be eligible for additional benefits or may have less options.

The law is meant to assure that foreign nationals who are permitted to live in the US, known as LPRs, will not be an economic burden to the government or taxpayers.

Those who are sponsored by an employer are guaranteed a salary equal to or greater than the prevailing wage given to anyone else for the same position. Similarly, US citizens or LPRs who sponsor their relatives must guarantee that they will support them financially if the relative is unable to support himself or herself.

The document that the US citizen signs is known as the Affidavit of Support (Form I-864).

As mentioned above, an Affidavit of Support is dissolved only when:

- **The foreign national can prove 40 quarters or 10 years of work;**
- **The foreign national or his or her sponsor dies; or**

- **The foreigner becomes a US citizen.**

Even when a couple divorces, the sponsoring spouse remains responsible for fulfilling this contract. If the foreign national does not want to apply for citizenship for two decades, it is unlikely that the soon to be ex-spouse can convince them to do it, unless discussed early in the divorce process, or perhaps as a negotiating point in the marital settlement agreement.

Your divorce clients may not realize the effects a separation (legal or in fact) may have on their immigration status, the status of their soon to be ex-spouse, or the immigration status of their children. By asking your client: "Is your spouse already a US citizen?" or "Are you already a US citizen?" you may advise an entirely different timeline or strategy.

If the couple is still married and living together, the LPR can apply for citizenship within three years (actually, two years and nine months) after getting the green card. However, if the couple divorces or separates, the foreign spouse will need to wait five years to apply for citizenship through naturalization.

The spouse seeking the divorce may not initially realize that the very best path is for the foreign national to become a US citizen as quickly as possible. Despite the often-challenging arrangement of remaining under one roof when a marriage has ended, the financial and personal results may be well worth the sacrifice.

When an LPR visits to learn about getting a divorce after being an LPR for three years, the family law attorney supplies the information about the divorce process.

The informed family law attorney will also share that:

- **The LPR does not abandon rights to their marital home if the couple separates;**
- **The foreign-born potential new client could face consequences to his or her immigration status; and**
- **Perhaps a recommendation to visit an immigration attorney.**

When clients fail to follow the advice of their attorney, and the LPR leaves the marital home rather than remaining under one roof together, an additional two-year wait time is automatically imposed. This means the LPR cannot apply for citizenship for at least two more years. There are far fewer employment opportunities for LPRs than there are for US citizens. These individuals suffer thousands in lost wages because of these decisions.

When an immigration attorney focusing on families is involved from the beginning the outcomes can be vastly different. When a couple consisting of a US Citizen and an LPR are mulling a split, the advice offered by an immigration attorney could be to delay the divorce. While married, the LPR who has been married and living with their US citizen spouse is eligible for citizenship. The US citizen spouse signed an Affidavit of Support when applying for LPR status for the foreign national spouse pledging to be financially responsible for the spouse for a very long time unless the wife becomes a US citizen. The family law attorney equipped with the correct information advises the couple to apply for citizenship for the foreign-born spouse while they are still married.

This remedy preserves the foreign-born spouse's status while releasing the US citizen from the affidavit of support once the spouse's citizenship is approved. When these steps have been taken, the couple may proceed to separate and complete their plans to divorce.

Three

Child Support and Immigration

Supporting children born to the marriage is a court-order that requires a spouse to pay the ex-spouse for the care and maintenance of a child. Immigration consequences may result for failure to pay this lawful obligation. Any foreign-born spouse who was ordered to pay child support yet fails to comply, may be ineligible for immigration benefits, including citizenship.

Those who pursue naturalization in the US must be LPRs first and must have maintained good moral character for a five-year period. Married LPRs must only meet a three-year requirement. Behaviors that challenge this good moral character may be repeated alcohol consumption; some types of arrests; interfering in others' marriages or causing a divorce; failing to pay taxes; or failing to pay child support. Immigration officials judge these behaviors with an extremely subjective rule.

For example, in Florida and some other states no ground needs to be specified to petition for divorce other than irreconcilable differences; however, adding adultery to the petition may affect the immigration status of the spouse. Likewise, if representing the responding party, objecting to that claim may save their immigration status.

Failing to understand child support implications can play havoc with your client's immigration goals. A person who does not understand these child support obligations relative to immigration rules may fall short on payments or abandon them altogether. A family law attorney who is not informed about immigration may advise the client that they are working to complete the divorce quickly and he or she can seek a modification of support from the courts later.

Following the divorce, the couple falls into a routine where child support payments become irregular or fall to the wayside and neither former spouse fusses about it. Sadly, years later, when this LPR parent applies for citizenship, he or she is questioned about marriage and children. Proof will be requested of the child support payments made throughout the years and the foreign-born parent cannot supply it and will no longer be eligible for citizenship.

Family law attorneys with a clear picture of immigration consequences advise clients with immigration goals completely differently.

The informed family law attorney would:

- **Advise the client to organize financial obligations around child support so that he or she may easily prove every payment;**
- **Explains to the client that while naturalization may not be an immediate goal, if these obligations are avoided now, citizenship will not be possible later;**
- **Advises that failure to pay ordered child support may also inhibit the foreign national's ability to secure LPR status;**

- A clean record of paying child support also bolsters good moral character as necessary evidence to avoid deportation; and
- Helps the client understand that child support is required even when the foreign national does not have the lawful ability to work in the US.

Four

Citizenship for Children Once There is Legal Custody

Some US citizens gain their citizenship by being born in the US to foreign parents a process called "deriving citizenship".

> **The Child Citizenship of 2000 allows foreign-born children to acquire US citizenship automatically when these conditions are met:**
>
> - **One or both parents is a US citizen by birth or naturalization;**
> - **The child is under 18-years-old; and**
> - **The child lives in the US or has lived in the US in the lawful and physical custody of the US citizen parent.**

This law permits a foreign-born child to become a US citizen *on the day that his or her parent becomes a US citizen*. A divorce can wreck this entire process. Here's how

The term "custody" — whether it is referring to joint custody, shared custody etc. — was eliminated in 2008 through changes in legislation.

It is now appropriate to use parental responsibility, sole parental responsibility, or shared parental responsibility. Outside of Florida, the term custody is still commonly used.

If the court does not give parental responsibility of the child or children to both parents, only to the LPR parent, the threat of harm is real. The only way to avoid this threat is to understand that at least some physical custody must be awarded to the US citizen parent in the official divorce documents.

For example, a couple, a US citizen and an LPR, want to file for divorce. The US citizen mother travels for work so does not seek physical custody, only visitation. Without the advice of a family immigration attorney explaining the unintended consequences, the child automatically loses the benefit of becoming a US citizen under the 2000 Child Citizenship Act. Instead, the child must wait until he or she is age 18 to apply for citizenship, which is a longer, more costly process. Had the couple been advised to agree to both having physical custody, the child could have secured citizenship by applying for a US passport directly with the Department of State.

This scenario is frequent and arises all too often. A common version is when a US citizen and a foreign person marry and the mother and child remain outside the US. When parents begin turning their thoughts to higher education, they seek potential immigration benefits to help their children pay tuition as though they lived in the US. All too often, as we review the divorce documents we learn that the father was not awarded any physical custody rights. Sadly, the child must pursue citizenship on his or her own.

Had the father been advised to seek at least partial physical custody, the entire situations would have been avoided. Unfortunately, this will result in cost of lost opportunity, in terms of money paid for higher education (as a foreign student instead of US citizen) and time delays in entering secondary education (waiting to be 21 to apply on their own, or waiting for the immigration process to complete), all leading to lost employment opportunities for the children, whether in the US or abroad.

Five

Divorce Prior to Removal of Conditions

A foreign national who marries a US citizen or LPR can obtain lawful permanent residency in the US. There are different rules as to how long it will take for a foreign national to obtain a green card based on who they marry and whether they are still outside the US.

If the couple has been married for less than two years on the day the foreign national receives lawful permanent residency, the process is not over. The foreign national is now a CPR, a Conditional Permanent Resident. There is a second step known as Removal of Conditions.

After the foreign national files for the initial green card, he or she obtains conditional permanent residency, a status with a two-year limit. The couple must take the final step of applying for removal of conditions; failure to do so may result in the foreign national being placed in removal proceedings. USCIS generally notifies the couple by mail explaining the critical nature of this step. The consequences of failing to take that step are also impressed upon the foreign national at the immigration interview, where he or she is required to sign a document stating they were advised to apply for removal of conditions.

After receiving the two-year residency, the couple must wait about a year and a half before proceeding to the second step. They must prepare during this time by continuously gathering evidence that they entered the marriage intending to build a life together, by demonstrating that they have made joint financial decisions, rented apartments, bought vehicles together and completing other typical, longer-term goals.

If the marriage is continuing and they live together, they may move ahead to the next step which is *jointly* filing the Removal of Conditions (Form I-751) within 90 days of their two-year anniversary of obtaining the green card.

Of course, some marriages end in divorce before two years. Some couples have such problems during the first year of marriage that they are at least thinking about divorce way before the two-year deadline has expired. These foreign nationals then turn to family law attorneys.

Family law attorneys who are not fully informed about immigration issues could overlook the status of a client who is a CPR. Too often, the advising attorney is not aware of the immigration consequences of a CPR's divorce and that without taking certain specific steps, he or she could be put in deportation proceedings and be ordered to leave the US.

On the other hand, the family law attorney who is informed about immigration and its relationship to divorce, counsels a CPR or LPR client differently. Instead of advising the client to move forward with the divorce, the first question this attorney will ask is: "How long has the client been a resident of the US and has the client already filed for Removal of Conditions?"

When you learn that your client's green card is set to expire in a few months, yet no Form I-751 has been filed, you should then shift the questioning to whether the client wants to file for the divorce soon.

The client must make this decision right away because Form I-751 must be filed within the three-month period prior to the couple's two-year anniversary; any time after the divorce is completed; or at any time if the couple is still married but there is abuse. As such, please note that to file a joint petition the couple must still be married and living together, and to file a waiver (of the joint requirement) I-751 petition, the couple's divorce must be final (not filed, pending, etc.).

If your client decides the divorce is what he really wants, his best move is to complete the divorce before that two-year deadline arrives so that deportation is avoided. If there is minimal contesting about joint property, the client can begin a quick divorce, finalize it prior to the two-year deadline, and then file Form I-751.

Sadly, when family law attorneys leave the immigration questions out of the equation, the likely result is their own client being placed in removal proceedings.

The Question of Abuse

When abuse is involved in a marriage, more challenges involving immigration and divorce are piled on. Abusers are known to use power and control to manipulate their victims.

If the spouse who is victimized begins threatening to leave or divorce, the abuser can soon feel threatened that they may be losing their upper hand and could increase their power and control tactics.

The result can be that the abuser begins applying tactics that he or she hopes will slow down the divorce process because the foreign national victim will need to self-petition for Removal of Conditions.

The knowledgeable family law attorney can address this best through a Motion to Bifurcate. The order terminates the marriage but maintains the jurisdiction within the family court so that property division or child care issues can be decided later.

The Question of Domestic Violence

If the foreign national is the abuser and there is a restraining order against them or criminal charges have been filed for domestic assault, battery, spousal or child abuse, stalking, harassment, etc., the foreign national's status is in jeopardy. It will affect their ability to remain in the US or reenter the US after a trip abroad.

What may seem minor based on state law may not be considered minor under federal immigration law. An immigrant convicted of a domestic violence crime is deportable, regardless of how long he or she has had lawful status in the country so long as the crime was committed after the individual was admitted to the country. This includes any conviction of child abuse, child neglect, child abandonment or stalking.

The term "domestic violence" refers to a crime of violence involving a current spouse, former spouse, live-in partner, co-parent, or any other individual by family law.

The term "violence" is defined in another immigration law section, but is either an offense involving an element of the use, attempted use or threatened use of physical force against another individual or the property of that other individual or a felony offense that involves a substantial risk of physical force against the individual or the individual's property by its very nature.

When a person has alleged domestic violence, he or she may secure an order of protection. Violating this protection order can make an immigrant deportable even if the underlying defense would not have done so.

Six

Employment-Based Residency: Green Card Despite Separation

Separation and divorce also can affect the foreign spouse's ability to obtain lawful permanent residency even when the immigration case is based on employment.

For instance, there are several categories of immigration status that awards a foreign worker permanent residency because an employer in the US needs the services of that person. This would include all family members including children under age 21. The processing of these cases can go on for many years before completed. When the foreign person has many years of experience or has a high level of education credentials, he or she typically receives residency somewhat faster.

When both spouses are foreign nationals and either visits a family law attorney to discuss divorce, problems lurk. Neither spouse is filing an immigration petition for the other so it may appear that there is no conflict. Once again, making a point to ask the couple about any pending immigration matters is critical. If that immigration questions goes unasked, the divorce proceedings may continue. To do so, can be a major error.

Let's say the couple is separated but still married, and that the husband has been petitioned by his employer for a green card. While the immigration process is pending, the wife is still eligible to obtain her green card through her husband *even though they are separated,* as long as they are not divorced.

Here again, a Motion to Bifurcate may be a good option. Likewise, a Petition for Support Unrelated to Divorce should be considered.

However, both spouses are better served by putting the divorce on hold at least until his wife can obtain her green card as well. This way, if she is living lawfully in the US and can work because she has her green card, the wife can make child support payments and see the children.

But let's say that the wife does not obtain her green card because they got divorced when they should not have, she will need to leave the US, with or without the children. In either instance, one parent will not have easy access to the see the children regularly or will be unable to pay child support.

Further, the children's status may be adversely affected and neither wife no children may be able to come visit the US for years, if ever, depending on where the breakdown in the process happened.

Seven

Residency Based on Non-Physical Relationship Trauma (VAWA)

The Violence Against Women Act (VAWA) is among the least used methods. Even though the law applies to both women and men, its name may prevent more people from utilizing its permissions.

When marriage goes wrong and one spouse who is a US Citizen or an LPR commits acts that are extremely cruel physically or mentally, VAWA may be used to obtain lawful permanent residency for the foreign national.

Survivors of such extreme abuse can petition for lawful permanent residency on their own. Anyone who can reasonably state that he or she has been the spouse of an abuser may try this route. In addition to battery and physical harm, mental cruelty may be used for a successful case.

Some examples of mental cruelty include:

- **Humiliation in public;**
- **Intimidation and degradation;**
- **Threat of harm to spouse or others;**
- **Threatening a spouse with deportation;**
- **Saying that he or she will commit suicide;**

- **Preventing the foreign national from getting a job or taking from them money earned;**
- **Social isolation or forced detention, and others.**

This is one more instance that involving the immigration conversation in the mix can mean everything to a case. A two-year deadline is in place for VAWA cases. If the victim spouse files for divorce and is granted it, the person *must* apply for lawful permanent residency no later than two years after divorcing the abuser.

When information of abuse is exposed along with immigration implications, the family law attorney can offer the client an opportunity to prepare to remain in the US by filing during or after the divorce because of the abuse element. This is such an important petition that the use of an immigration attorney should not be side-stepped.

Eight

Spouse of a Temporary Worker During Separation or Divorce

When a foreign national is married to another foreign national who is in the US on a work visa, separation or divorce presents a host of problems.

Some spouses are authorized to work; however, that authorization is only in place when they are the dependent of a multinational manager or executive, or an investor. If the marriage ends, so does that spouse's status and work permit. What is worse is that there *is no grace period*! This spouse cannot work one single day after the divorce is finalized, nor can he or she remain in the US.

Because the consequences can be so immediate, informed family law attorneys should advise the client to delay the divorce until spouse has obtained his or her own status.

For example, if an investor and his/her spouse are working towards a divorce, the divorce should not be finalized until the investor's spouse has obtained a new status. Student status is often advised as the easiest status to seek. The potential student must process a visa outside the US, but only after the school has admitted the potential student. This may not work if admission is not set to start or if the person has not completed sufficient education, or simply does not want to pursue any further education. If this option will not work, consider other options.

If the investor's spouse has the same citizenship as the investor (or another citizenship allowing for investor visas), she can become an investor in her own right. The funds to start the new business would come from the expected distribution of properties upon divorce.

Although it is not necessary to have the new business up and running to obtain an investor visa, the funds would need to be available prior to the issuance of the visa.

Nine

Adoption Before the Sixteenth Birthday

When you want to adopt a foreign-born child, the key thing to know is to get the actual adoption decree before the child turns 16. Immigration benefits are only available to adopted foreign children if they are adopted before they reach that age. An exception to this rule is that a sibling of an adopted child may still be eligible for immigration benefits if he or she is younger than age 18 at the time of the adoption.

Just as requirements exist for married couples, so are there requirements for the adopted foreign child. The adopted child must live with a US Citizen or LPR for two years and the parent must have legal custody of that child throughout that period as well.

At times, a decree is required from family court demonstrating that the parent has had legal custody for two years. The rules permit the two-year residence requirement to begin *before* the child is adopted. So, if a parent has legal custody of a child for several years, more than two, and then files for adoption, the two-year requirement is fulfilled.

When learning about the relationship between immigration and adoption, understanding the powerful connection between the two is vital, because a person adopted by a US citizen or LPR parent enjoys all the benefits that a natural-born child of any parent would enjoy.

When the adopting family has had two years of joint residency with the child as well as two years of legal custody, the family can often get an adoption decree even after the child has become an adult, *nunc pro tunc.*

When the *nunc pro tunc* decree is issued by the court after the foreign-born person is an adult, the legal consequences mirror those of children adopted before age 16. Thanks to the Child Citizenship Act of 2000, a foreign-born child could potentially obtain immediate citizenship from a US citizen parent if this *nunc pro tunc* decree is sought.

Thank you for your interest in learning more about how to help your clients.

We are available to help advise you and your clients on simple as well as more complicated immigration matters.

Case Evaluation

954-357-0957

About the Author:
Connie Kaplan, Esq.

Attorney Connie Kaplan graduated from the State University of New York with a Bachelor of Science degree in Business, *summa cum laude*. She then went on to receive her law degree from Nova Southeastern University. While attending Nova Southeastern University, she received the Goodwin Scholarship, was on the dean's list, and graduated with honors. She also served as the Editor-in-Chief of the ILSA Journal for International and Comparative Law. She has since returned to the Shepard Broad College of Law at Nova Southeastern University as an Adjunct Professor of Law.

Notes:

Notes:

www.ingramcontent.com/pod-product-compliance
Lightning Source LLC
Chambersburg PA
CBHW072300170526
45158CB00003BA/1131